Ellie Stewart

Two Plays

Hope and Joy & The Return

Salamander Street

PLAYS

First published in 2020 by Salamander Street Ltd.
(info@salamanderstreet.com)

Hope and Joy & *The Return* © Ellie Stewart, 2020

ISBN: 9781913630027

Printed and bound in Great Britain

10 9 8 7 6 5 4 3 2 1

CONTENTS

The Return is a playful reimagining of real events surrounding a trial for imposture in 1560 in the South West of France. It is not faithful to any historical account of the events. I gratefully acknowledge as inspiration the writing of Natalie Zemon Davis (*The Return of Martin Guerre*, 1983) and Jean Coras (*Arrest Memorable du parlement de Tolose*, 1561).

Hope and Joy was written over several years. Winning the Tron Theatre Progressive Playwright Award was a key stage in its development.

Heartfelt thanks goes to the extended network of people who made the writing of these plays possible, and special thanks to Philip Howard and Caitlin Skinner for making exciting things happen.

Ellie Stewart, May 2020

Hope and Joy

a Pearlfisher and Stellar Quines commission

Hope and Joy, produced by Stellar Quines and Pearlfisher, was first performed on Friday 25 October 2019, Cumbernauld Theatre, before embarking on a Scottish tour.

HOPE	Kim Gerard
JOY	Beth Marshall
MAGNUS	Ryan Havelin

Creative Team

Director	Caitlin Skinner
Set and Costume Designer	Becky Minto
Lighting Designer	Emma Jones
Sound Designer	Susan Bear
Movement Director	Amy Kennedy
Movement Direction Mentor	Christine Devaney
Stage Manager	Sophie Wright

Characters

HOPE
female (between 20 and 40)

JOY
female (between 40 and 60)

MAGNUS
male (age 16/17)

PART 1

The beating wings of a large bird increase in frequency and decrease in volume until it sounds like a foetal heartbeat.

***

Summer.

A room in a hospital.

HOPE *is in labour. She's in the middle of a contraction. She is groaning.*

JOY *is supporting her physically.*

JOY: Keep moving. Keep breathing. You're doing great.

    A wee while. The contraction passes.

JOY: There you go. That's better, isn't it?

    First time?

HOPE: Last.

JOY: They all say that.

    Till the next time.

    What are you having?

HOPE: What am I having?

JOY: Girl or boy?

HOPE: I don't know. It's … unexpected.

JOY: One night stand?

    Beat.

HOPE: Kind of.

JOY: Pished were you?

HOPE: No!

    Pause.

HOPE: It was …

I think there might be complications.

JOY looks at HOPE's notes.

JOY: Nothing in your notes, Hope.

HOPE: No. I didn't …

But I think it might be …

I don't know what to expect.

JOY looks at the notes.

JOY: None of us knows what to expect.

Pause.

HOPE: The circumstances of conception were … unusual.

JOY: None of our business how the wean got in there. The main thing is, it gets out safe.

HOPE: I think it might be a wee bit unique.

JOY: Look, if you've got a medical history just write it in your notes.

JOY passes the notes to HOPE.

JOY: Write it in some kind of squiggly handwriting – makes it look like a Doctor's.

HOPE: I can write my own notes?

JOY: Somebody has to. No one else has time. But do it quick before the next contraction.

Too late. The contraction has started.

JOY: Is the Father coming in?

HOPE breathing. Shakes her head.

JOY: Anyone you can call?

HOPE groaning

JOY: Girlfriend?

HOPE groaning

JOY: Mum?

HOPE *groaning.*

JOY: Pal?

The contraction is passing.

JOY: You won't be long now. That's my shift finished.

HOPE: What?

JOY: I don't get overtime for this.

HOPE: But I don't know what's happening!

JOY: You must have some idea.

HOPE: No!

HOPE *shakes her head.*

JOY: From the telly?

HOPE: No.

JOY: You'll be fine. There are four born every second. *(Claps four times quickly.)* Just like that.

HOPE: Not like this one.

JOY: You'll be fine.

HOPE: When does the next midwife start?

JOY: Midwife?

They don't call a midwife till you're at least seven centimetres dilated.

If it all goes to plan you probably won't even see a midwife.

HOPE: But you're a midwife.

JOY: I'm not even an auxiliary. I'm just the cleaner.

But I'll get someone to bring you a nice cup of tea and a biscuit. Plenty of sugar.

HOPE: I don't take sugar. It makes me sick.

JOY: You'll be sick anyway. At least you'll have something to bring up.

***

JOY *at home. She is on the sofa with a goldfish in a bowl. She has a bag of crisps.*

She talks to the goldfish.

JOY: What do you think? Flying Doctors? How to Train Your Hamster? Grand Designs?

…

I know, it's not your favourite.

…

It is a special though … it's on stilts.

JOY *opens the bag of crisps and crumbles a wee bit of crisp into the goldfish bowl.*

JOY: ¡Que aproveche!

Banging on the wall from the next room.

JOY *puts the bowl down.*

JOY: *(To goldfish.)* Don't go away.

***

The next day in the hospital room. **HOPE** *and* **JOY**. **JOY** *is cleaning.*

HOPE *tries to move. She winces.*

JOY: Sore, are you?

HOPE: Only when I move. Or cough. Or pee. It's worst when I pee.

JOY: You should pee in the shower. It really helps. You have to …

JOY *mimes hosing her own fanny with a shower head.*

JOY: But it really helps.

HOPE: How long does it last?

JOY: Which bit?

HOPE: The stingy as fuck bit.

JOY: Not long.

Pause.

HOPE: Are they talking about me?

JOY: A bit.

HOPE: What are they saying?

JOY: That you're a grunter.

HOPE: A grunter?

JOY: Don't worry about it. Everyone does something. There's the grunters, the honkers, the growlers, the beaters, the screamers, the whoopers, the greeters, the ones that bellow, the ones that low.

You are a grunter.

Beat.

HOPE: It's not what I expected.

JOY: They all say that. I don't know what they expect.

HOPE: Well I wasn't expecting … an egg.

JOY: An egg?

HOPE: No one's saying anything but it's clearly an egg.

JOY: An egg?

    JOY *looks in the incubator.*

JOY: Oh.

    So it is.

    HOPE *looks at* **JOY**.

JOY: It's a beautiful egg.

HOPE: Is it?

JOY: Gorgeous.

    They look at the egg.

    JOY *starts talking to it in a high pitched voice.*

JOY: Are you coming out? Are you? Are you?

    JOY *makes cooing noises to the egg.*

HOPE: Joy. I've had an egg.

JOY: It still likes regular baby stuff.

    (To the egg) You like that sort of thing.

    Don't you?

    Yes you do.

    Yes you do.

    Beat.

JOY: Go on … give it a cuddle.

    HOPE *won't take the egg*

HOPE: I'm scared I might drop it.

JOY: Course you won't drop it.

    Pause.

HOPE: I'm scared I might drop it deliberately.

    JOY *puts the egg gently back in the incubator.*

HOPE: What if we don't bond. What if it's ugly?

JOY: Oh it'll be ugly all right. Newborns are always ugly. But you won't think it's ugly.

    Pause.

HOPE: But it's … different.

JOY: Hope doll, it is hatching out of an egg. There is a strong chance that it's going to be different. But all it'll need is love … and somewhere to spread its wings.

HOPE: How do you know that?

JOY: Eh?

HOPE: How do you know it'll have wings?

JOY: What?

HOPE: 'Somewhere to spread its wings'?

JOY: That's just something people s…

    Beat.

JOY: It's going to have actual wings?

A big moment.

JOY: It was a bird?

...

A biggish bird?

HOPE: ...

JOY: Goose?

HOPE *shakes her head.*

JOY: Stork?

A look. (Do you think you're funny?)

JOY: Swan?

HOPE: Whooper Swan.

A moment.

JOY: What was he like?

HOPE: They're bigger than a Mute Swan, and the beak's a bit more pointy.

JOY: I actually meant the sex. What was the sex like?

HOPE: It was ... fine.

JOY: ...

HOPE: He was ... unbelievably graceful.

JOY: Unbelievably graceful? There's a thing you don't hear every day.

So where is he now?

HOPE: Langisjór in Southern Iceland. Sixty-four degrees, ten minutes and one second North, Eighteen degrees, nineteen minutes, fourteen seconds West.

I'm tracking him with a forty gramme solar powered satellite transmitter.

A look from **JOY**.

HOPE: Oh ... I'm not stalking him.

It's my job.

At least it was my job.

Researching the impact of climate change on the migratory habits of Icelandic Whooper Swans.

…

I was meant to be going to Iceland. To visit the Highland Meadows.

JOY: Maybe he'll come back and see you.

HOPE: I doubt it. Last year they nearly didn't come back at all.

A moment.

JOY *takes the egg out the incubator.*

JOY: Here … have a wee cuddle in.

HOPE: What if I crush it? What if I roll over and it falls out the bed?

She gives the egg to **HOPE**.

JOY: Here.

See?

It's like a wee warm stone, eh?

***

JOY *at home with her goldfish. Her mother is in the next room. She takes a shopping list from her pocket. Reads.*

JOY: Fish food.

Paracetamol.

Daz.

Neutradol.

Tomato soup.

Tomato soup.

She adds 'stain remover' to her list.

JOY: Stain remover.

Potatoes.

Milk.

Bread.

Eggs.

…

Crosses out 'eggs'.

Beer.

Crisps.

Banging on the wall.

JOY: OK Mum, OK.

***

Morning. **HOPE** *has a knitting pattern, a circular needle and a tangle of wool. She's distraught.*

JOY: What are you doing?

HOPE: I don't know. I've never used a circular needle before.

JOY: Well what's it supposed to be?

HOPE: It's an egg warmer. Apparently it's not safe to have him in the bed beside me.

JOY: Who told you that?

HOPE: The experts.

  JOY *picks up the knitting pattern and rips it up.*

HOPE: Now I'll never know what I'm doing!

JOY: *(Shouts.)* None of us knows what we're doing Hope!

  Least of all the experts!

  A moment.

JOY: Sorry. I'm really sorry. I haven't slept. I think I'm losing it.

  Pause.

HOPE: I can ask the psychologists for a questionnaire if you like.

  To see if you're feeling shite.

JOY: I can tell when I'm feeling shite.

HOPE: They'll be able to tell how shite you feel … a wee bit shite or a big bit shite. And if you've always felt shite. Apparently I'm feeling shiter than before but not clinically shite.

JOY: You'll feel different when it hatches.

Beat.

JOY: Do you smoke cannabis?

HOPE: No!

JOY: Pity.

Do you have a bath?

HOPE: Shower.

JOY: You'll need to get a bath put in. It's the next best thing after cannabis. And probably better for you in the long run.

HOPE: How do you relax?

JOY: Give my mum a sleeping tablet, open a bottle of beer and watch 'So You Want to Be a Midwife'.

HOPE: 'So You Want to Be a Midwife'? Is that a thing?

JOY: It's like 'So You Think You Can Dance' meets 'The Apprentice' meets 'DIY NHS'.

'I liked the way Team A handled the ventouse, but let's face it, they really fucked up on the stitches.'

HOPE: Ouch.

JOY: It sounds better on the telly.

HOPE: You should go on. You'd be great.

JOY: Pedro's not keen. He thinks I should have stuck in at school and been a real midwife.

HOPE: It's never too late.

JOY: I thought about it, but you need Higher English.

HOPE: You should go for it. You show Pedro it's never too late.

Pause.

HOPE: They want to do tests.

JOY: What for?

HOPE: I don't know. I don't think they know.

JOY: They'll probably all want a bit of him right enough. To prove how clever they are.

The room is suddenly too small for **HOPE**.

A moment.

JOY: Here … give me that knitting.

Exit **JOY**.

***

JOY *at home. Her goldfish is beside her. Her mother is in the next room. She reads a letter.*

JOY: Dear Service User, in line with the government's independent living reforms, we are reducing your mother's care package from seven minutes to four minutes a day. This does not apply at weekends or on public holidays when no service is provided.

JOY *puts the letter in her pocket.*

JOY: *(To goldfish.)*: ¿Qué vamos a hacer?

JOY *picks up the knitting.*

Banging on the wall from the next room.

***

The egg hatches.

***

The hospital room. The next morning. Enter **JOY**.

JOY: So … ?

HOPE: So?

JOY: So … what is it?

HOPE: It's got wings.

Webbed toes.

Slight fusion of the nose and jaw, but not so you'd notice.

JOY: Is it a girl or a boy?

JOY looks in the incubator.

HOPE: Boy.

JOY: Oh my! Look at you! You are GORGEOUS!

(To the baby.) You are gorgeous. Yes you are. Aren't you gorgeous? Did you tap your way out? Did you? Did you?

HOPE: The tapping thing is a myth. They uncurl.

JOY: *(To the baby.)* Aw that is cute. Isn't that cute?

HOPE: It's actually quite messy.

JOY: Can I hold him?

HOPE: If you like.

JOY lifts the baby.

JOY: *(To the baby)* You are lovely. Aren't you?

What's your name?

What's your name?

What is your name?

JOY looks to HOPE.

HOPE: I thought maybe Magnus?

JOY: *(To the baby.)* You look like a Magnus. Yes you do. You look like a Magnus.

HOPE: He looks like an alien.

Pause.

JOY: *(To HOPE.)* Are you OK?

HOPE: It's not all it's cracked up to be, is it?

Pause.

JOY: Here.

JOY *gives* **HOPE** *the baby to hold.*

HOPE *holds the baby.*

JOY: Look at you.

You will both be grand.

Trust me.

A moment.

The baby starts crying. A miauling cry – like a cat. Or a seagull.

HOPE: He's hardly stopped crying since he hatched.

JOY: Have you tried a dummy?

HOPE: They said it's not good for him.

JOY: If it's good for you, it's good for him.

She takes a dummy out of her pocket and puts it in the baby's mouth.

He stops crying.

HOPE: How long will he cry for?

JOY: Ear plugs are good. Industrial ear protectors are better.

HOPE: I can't even hold him right.

JOY: New babies are hard to hold.

JOY *takes the baby.*

JOY: Especially when they've got wings.

HOPE: He looks like a pterosaurus. Hundreds of thousands years of human evolution and I get a pterosaurus.

JOY: Aye. Hundreds of thousands years and look where it got us!

(To the baby.) You are lovely. Aren't you? Yes you are.

HOPE: They won't let me out till they've done the tests. But they don't know when they can do the tests. I don't think they even know what they're testing for.

JOY: Has anyone even asked about his father?

HOPE *shakes her head.*

JOY: Geez.

HOPE: And he's under the weight threshold. I tried telling them that his bones are probably hollow. That maybe he needs a supplement of algae and tadpoles. But that's not part of their post-natal care package.

JOY: You are going to be a great mum.

HOPE: Do you think?

JOY: Definitely.

...

But maybe you'd both be better off outside. He needs water and air and ....

HOPE: They say they can remove his wings straight away.

JOY: They what?!

HOPE: Apparently it's a simple operation if it's done early enough. And he could grow up more or less normal.

JOY: Normal?

HOPE: You know … so he fits in. Doesn't stand out.

JOY: Hope … everyone … at every time … in the whole of human history has dreamt of being able to fly and they want to remove his WINGS?

You will definitely be better off outside.

HOPE: I asked to go home. But they won't discharge me.

JOY signs HOPE's notes with a flourish.

JOY: There. Discharged.

HOPE: Won't you get into trouble?

JOY: Probably. And you'll have to go out the window.

JOY starts tying the baby to HOPE's front.

JOY: You'll have to be quick. They don't like people opening windows.

JOY is tying the baby to HOPE's front with a blanket.

JOY: Soon we'll all forget how to fall and jump and breathe.

...

There's a tree outside. If you sit on the sill you can reach the big branch and dreep down.

JOY unlocks the window.

JOY: OK?

HOPE: I'm not sure.

I don't really know what I'm doing.

JOY: Most things aren't that complicated.

…

Ready?

JOY opens the window. An alarm sounds.

Blackout.

PART 2

Five years later. Spring.

HOPE *and* **MAGNUS** *are outside, playing a game. They are telling each other jokes. They have both heard them all before.*

HOPE: Why did the chicken/

MAGNUS: Yeah yeah. Why did the duck cross the road?

HOPE: Because it thought it was a chicken.

   …

   Why did the fish cross the ocean?

MAGNUS: To get to the other tide.

   …

   Why did the rooster cross the road?

HOPE: To prove it wasn't chicken.

   …

   Wait … why did the dinosaur cross the road?

MAGNUS: Because the chicken wasn't around yet.

   …

   Which came first/ the chicken or

HOPE: The egg! By three hundred and twelve million years.

   HOPE *is tired. She sits.*

   MAGNUS *is above her. He unfurls his whole body. He's a head taller now. His neck is very long. With his arms extended to the sides he demonstrates scooping the air with his arms and shoulders.*

MAGNUS: I'll teach you to fly one day.

HOPE: You won't. It's not anatomically possible.

MAGNUS: Deep in everyone's DNA there's the possibility of flight.

HOPE: I do dream about flying sometimes.

MAGNUS: There you go then.

HOPE: It's just symbolic or something.

MAGNUS: Bollocks. It's your brain preparing for flight.

HOPE: Maybe.

MAGNUS: Birds were the only dinosaur to survive you know.

***

JOY at home. She is on the sofa with a goldfish in a bowl on her lap. She has a bundle of newspapers and a bag of crisps. She speaks to her goldfish (Pedro Dieciséis).

JOY reads the front page headlines aloud.

JOY: 'Woman sues NHS over Uneggspected Pregnancy'

...

'Quick Shag Takes on New Meaning for Coastal Holiday Makers – Lewd behaviour on Arran's beautiful beaches.'

...

'Woman gives birth to Albatross after Holiday of a Lifetime.'

...

Albatross? Must've had a bit of bother getting that one out.

...

What do you think? 'Gone With the Wind'?
Pause.

JOY: I know. Too long. No point.

She opens the bag of crisps and crumbles a little into the goldfish bowl.

JOY: ¡Que aproveche!

...

Wait for it.

JOY's mum does not bang from the next room.

A moment.

JOY: Mum.

It is very quiet. No sound from the next room. An absence of breathing.

***

MAGNUS *has a razor. He has been trying to shave his legs. It's messy. Enter* **HOPE**.

HOPE: Magnus!

MAGNUS: Why do you never knock?

HOPE: What is this?

MAGNUS: What does it look like?

Beat.

HOPE: Why?

Pause.

MAGNUS: Melissa says I'm …

She says I'm … fluffier than normal.

Down there.

…

She laughed.

HOPE: She was probably just nervous.

I'm sure I laughed the first time.

MAGNUS: I don't think it's her first time Mum. She said, 'Don't you even wax?'

HOPE: Wax?

Down there?

MAGNUS: Everyone's waxing.

And then we were learning how to prepare chicken and I felt sick so I / went to

HOPE: Wait a minute …

Melissa put her hand down your trousers in Food Tech?

MAGNUS: Don't be stupid. That would be totally unhygienic. Food Tech's straight after break.

HOPE: Right.

MAGNUS: I went to the school office and they tried to phone you but I had to go back to class.

HOPE: Shit!

   …

   Sorry Magnus.

MAGNUS: Do you know how they pluck birds?

   They scald the carcass in hot water and put it in a rotating drum with spikes. Then they singe the skin to get the fluff off.

   It smells terrible.

   Like burning hair.

HOPE: Oh Magnus … you shouldn't have to sit through that.

MAGNUS: Don't do anything, Mum. Don't go and complain or anything stupid like that.

HOPE: …

MAGNUS: It's no big deal and the teachers'll just laugh at me.

HOPE: The teachers laugh at you?

MAGNUS: They're always laughing at me.

   Pause.

MAGNUS: Please?

HOPE: OK.

MAGNUS: Promise?

   Pause.

MAGNUS: Do you think I should wax?

HOPE: I have no idea. But if Melissa's laughing at you then …

MAGNUS: I should wax.

HOPE: No. Maybe she's not right for you.

MAGNUS: Mum … please don't tell me what to do. You don't understand normal relationships.

***

MAGNUS *at the park bench. A seagull swoops down and circles the bench.* **MAGNUS** *looks under the bench and picks up a bag of seeds that the seagull has cached. Exit seagull.*

***

JOY *and her goldfish.* **JOY** *reads a letter.*

JOY: 'Cohabiting'?

…

Who with?

JOY: *(To Pedro.)* They've stopped my housing allowance.

Apparently I'm 'cohabiting'.

She pours a tiny drop of beer into the goldfish bowl.

JOY: Te gusta la cerveza.

…

Pedro, Pedro. ¿Qué vamos a hacer?

…

Te quiero mucho Pedro. ¿Sabes?

***

HOPE *at home, reading.*

HOPE: Fledging. Eight behaviours. Head up … preening … dipping … feeding on emergents … picking … grazing … drinking and roosting.

Picking … grazing … drinking … roosting.

Enter **MAGNUS**.

MAGNUS *runs at* **HOPE**, *arms out. He would swipe* **HOPE** *but she ducks at the last minute and he has to spin.*

He stops. She looks at him. She growls. A deep growl in her throat.

He hisses. He bites her left arm, and she grabs him.

They fight until they are exhausted.

MAGNUS: You said you wouldn't do anything.

HOPE: I couldn't just / let them

MAGNUS: I can't go back now.

HOPE: You have to go back! You've nearly finished your NQs!

MAGNUS: You shouldn't have said anything. It just makes it worse.

HOPE: It's not just about you! We have to speak up for everyone. The ones coming behind. The ones moving in. You're not the only one!

MAGNUS: You don't even care about me, do you?

HOPE: Magnus, I mushed worms for you. I put pondweed in your bath. I taught you to fly!

MAGNUS: Eh naw you never… you took me down the pond and left me with some random ducks.

HOPE: They were a nice family. They were Goldeneyes.

MAGNUS: You never even KNEW them!

Exit **MAGNUS**.

HOPE: Magnus!

MAGNUS: I'm not going back!

***

MAGNUS *at the park bench. He feeds seeds to a few pigeons. The pigeons are animated, and flock to him. There is a touch of fear in him, but mostly he likes it.*

JOY *arrives at the park bench. She has her goldfish in a bowl. She sits on the bench and makes herself at home. She starts feeding the ducks.*

MAGNUS *wasn't expecting anyone else to be here.*

MAGNUS: You shouldn't feed ducks bread.

JOY: There never even used to be a pond here.

JOY continues to feed the ducks.

MAGNUS: It's not good for them. It encourages algae/ and rats.

25

A seagull swoops on the goldfish bowl.

JOY: Get off my FISH!

> **JOY** *chases it off with a stick. She's violent.*

JOY: And don't come back!

> *Pause.*

JOY: What a gannet!

MAGNUS: He's a Black-headed Gull.

JOY: Vicious. Did you see his scars?

MAGNUS: It's hard for them now. There's not enough food to go round.

JOY: Are you kidding me? Have you not seen them down the chippy?
They don't know what a queue is.

MAGNUS: He's trying to put on weight for Málaga. It's a two thousand
kilometre flight.

JOY: Pals, are you?

MAGNUS: Kind of.

> *Pause.*

JOY: How old are you now?

> …

> In Swan years.

> *Pause.*

MAGNUS: Do I know you?

JOY: I doubt it.

MAGNUS: … ?

JOY: I knew your mother.

MAGNUS: … ?

JOY: I worked in the hospital.

> When you were …

> When you …

26

MAGNUS: Right.

...

Look ... are you going to be here for long?

JOY *shrugs.*

JOY: Maybe forever.

She looks at the goldfish bowl.

They didn't realise Pedro is a fish. They thought I was cohabiting and stopped my payments.

MAGNUS: Can't you get a room somewhere?

JOY: Now they know Pedro's a fish I'm not a priority on the homeless register. Cause it's strictly no pets.

They sit, saying nothing.

JOY: Meeting someone?

MAGNUS: Kind of.

...

Well I was.

JOY: Do you want me to pass on a message?

MAGNUS: Nah. You're all right. I'll catch him later.

MAGNUS *is leaving.*

JOY: Tell your mum that Joy was asking for her.

JOY *goes back to feeding the ducks.*

***

Pigeon party at the flat. Pigeons everywhere. **MAGNUS** *in the middle of it. They finish the seeds.*

***

The next morning. **HOPE** *at the flat. Scrubbing bird droppings off the floor. Enter* **MAGNUS**.

HOPE: What is this?

MAGNUS: I don't know.

HOPE: It's like bird droppings.

MAGNUS: Are you accusing me of shitting on the floor?

HOPE: Of course not! I'm just …

> *Beat.*

HOPE: Maybe I left the window open.

> **MAGNUS** *is leaving* **HOPE** *scrubs.*

HOPE: *(Low.)* Pigeon shit. Oh joy.

MAGNUS: *(Low.)* Shit!

> **MAGNUS** *turns.*

MAGNUS: There's this woman sleeping down the park. Says she knows you.

> Joy … from the hospital?

> *Exit* **MAGNUS**.

> **HOPE** *stops scrubbing.*

HOPE: Joy?

> …

> Joy.

> *Exit* **HOPE**.

***

The same day. **HOPE** *and* **JOY** *enter the flat.*

HOPE: Sorry about the smell.

JOY: It is kind of airless. Maybe you could open a window.

HOPE: I have to keep the windows shut. Or the Pigeons come in.

JOY: Come in?

HOPE: I don't know … I think Magnus is …

> It's so difficult.

JOY: Well no one said it would be easy.

HOPE: All he'll need is love, you said.

JOY: Did I say that?

Pause.

JOY: What are you doing now? Still researching Whooper Swans.

HOPE: Investigating the impact of wind farms on the flight paths of Pink-footed Geese.

JOY: Do you get paid for that?

HOPE: I'm still a government scientist.

But I'm back at level one.

I just have to count the geese.

JOY *looking round.*

JOY: Is there a room for Pedro?

HOPE: Pedro? Oh. I didn't realise …

I mean … no.

He'd have to sleep in here. But …

JOY *puts the bowl down.*

JOY: *(To Pedro.)* ¿Qué te parece, Pedro?

Beat.

HOPE: Wait a minute.

Pedro is the goldfish?

JOY: Of course Pedro is a goldfish. What is it with people?

HOPE: Pedro is the goldfish.

Beat.

HOPE: Right. OK.

JOY: Did you get a bath put in?

HOPE: Would you like a bath?

JOY: We would LOVE a bath.

(To Pedro.) Wouldn't we?

HOPE: Oh.

JOY: If it's not too much trouble?

HOPE: No of course not.

Just …

Aren't goldfish cold-blooded?

JOY: We've come to a compromise.

HOPE: Right. OK.

JOY: I just need one towel obviously.

HOPE: Yes.

Obviously.

JOY: This way?

Exit **JOY**.

HOPE: *(Shouts after her.)* Help yourself to … whatever …

***

The same day. **MAGNUS** *at the bench, waiting for Scarface the Seagull. Eventually the pigeons come.* **MAGNUS** *has no seeds to feed them. They are agitated.*

***

Late that night. **MAGNUS** *comes in from the park. He pours a glass of water from a jug and drinks it.*

MAGNUS: *(To Pedro.)* What are you looking at?

Are you flashing your tail at me?

I can wiggle too.

Look.

MAGNUS *wiggles.*

MAGNUS: Oh you like that?

Well I'm not doing it cause you like it.

I think I might head North.

Maybe Iceland.

Do you ever get that?

You just want to fly off?

I don't suppose you do.

You just have to go round.

And round.

And round.

Up there you can see everything.

The shape of the hills.

Where the valleys meet.

The traces of the riverbeds.

The lights on the motorway.

Like electrons.

Or blood.

***

Next day. **MAGNUS** *and* **HOPE** *are in the flat.* **JOY** *is in the bath. There is a tapping on the window.*

MAGNUS: I really need to pee.

HOPE: They're in the bath.

MAGNUS: Again?!

HOPE: They shouldn't be long now. They've been in for ages.

MAGNUS: Are they staying long?

HOPE: I don't know.

MAGNUS: *(Low.)* I mean that is not normal, is it?

HOPE: You're only young, Magnus. Life's not as straightforward as it
    seems. It's not always … logical.

    …

What is that tapping?

MAGNUS: It's probably just one of the pigeons.

HOPE *goes to the window.*

HOPE: Shoo!

...

I don't trust those pigeons. There's something about them.

MAGNUS: I tell you who I don't trust. I don't trust that goldfish. Beady eyes watching me all the time. Swimming round in circles. I think he's spying on me.

Enter **JOY**. *She is just out the bath. She carries Pedro in his bowl.* **MAGNUS** *doesn't see her.*

HOPE: He's not spying on you Magnus, it's what they do ... they just go round in circles in a small bowl.

JOY: You should get spikes put down.

MAGNUS: Spikes?

JOY: For the pigeons. There's dozens of them!

HOPE : Magnus ... what do they want?

JOY: They'll be wanting more of their special seeds.

HOPE: Seeds?

JOY: ...

MAGNUS: It's just poppy seeds.

But I've run out.

HOPE: I'm being held hostage in my own home because you've run out of poppy seeds?

JOY: Opium.

HOPE: You're a drug dealer?!

MAGNUS: Chill, Mum. It's not illegal to feed the birds. And it's a hard time for pigeons. They just need a wee hit to get them through.

JOY: It'll be that seagull. Scarface. Nicking them out the health food shop on the High Street. We've seen him.

HOPE: Who's Scarface?

MAGNUS: It's a few poppy seeds? What's the problem?

Beat.

HOPE: We'll need to report them.

MAGNUS: They're just getting a bit jumpy.

HOPE: They're addicted, Magnus!

Exit **HOPE**.

Glares between **JOY** *and* **MAGNUS**.

A moment.

Exit **MAGNUS**.

JOY *picks up the book that* **HOPE** *was reading.*

JOY: Lonely Planet Iceland.

...

Lonely Planet.

A moment.

She looks at Pedro.

***

The flat. Night-time. **MAGNUS** *enters. He is being chased by pigeons. Pedro is in his bowl on the table.*

MAGNUS *takes the bowl and drinks the water, swallowing Pedro whole.*

A moment.

***

The next morning. **HOPE** *and* **JOY**. **JOY** *has the empty bowl.*

JOY: He's gone.

HOPE: I know. I heard him come in last night, but he's not in his room.

JOY: What?

HOPE: He's hasn't slept in his bed.

JOY: Pedro! Pedro has gone!

HOPE: Are you sure?

JOY: Look!

HOPE: Gone?

   …

   How?

   Beat.

JOY: Magnus has eaten him.

HOPE: Oh stop it!

JOY: A swan would eat a small fish.

HOPE: He's not a swan!

JOY: He's half swan.

HOPE: He's my son and I didn't bring him up to eat other peoples' goldfish!

JOY: I heard him banging about last night. He probably had the munchies.

HOPE: He did not eat Pedro!

JOY: Magnus would eat anything. I've seen him.

HOPE: He's growing.

JOY: There you go then.

HOPE: Look … I KNOW he wouldn't eat Pedro. He doesn't even like goldfish.

JOY: I knew it. He never liked Pedro and now he's eaten him.

HOPE: He doesn't LIKE goldfish. He likes peanut butter sandwiches. He likes Cheerios. He likes Ben and Jerry's phish…

JOY: I'm right about this. You'll see.

   Exit **JOY**.

   The flat is suddenly very empty. Even the pigeons have gone.

MAGNUS *is flying North North West over Scotland.*

Scotland in Spring smells of slurry.

Petrol.

Incinerators, beer and kebabs.

Yeast.

Vomit.

Chips.

Burning heather.

Scones.

Seaweed.

Bog myrtle.

Fishing boats.

Peat smoke.

Mist and smirr and rain and / fog and …

The sound of a drone getting closer. (A military drone, not bagpipes.)

MAGNUS: Shit!

MAGNUS *is falling.*

Blackout.

***

JOY *at the bench. Enter* **HOPE**. *She sits on the bench. There is a long silence.*

HOPE: Listen … I don't know for sure … but I wonder if … I'm wondering if he's gone North for summer. If maybe he was fattening up for the flight and … ?

JOY: Figures.

It's what they do.

HOPE: I'm so sorry.

JOY: Hardly a headline … Swan Eats Fish.

HOPE: Still …

   Pause.

JOY: Anyway, I'll get another one. You'd think I'd learn, but I just make the same mistakes again. I'm full of good intentions. I say 'get a gerbil, Joy … or a guinea pig.' But goldfish are so SHINY.

   Pause.

JOY: Are you missing him?

HOPE: I'm enjoying the space.

JOY: You're feeling shite, aren't you?

HOPE: …

JOY: I can give you a questionnaire if you like. See how shite you feel.

HOPE: I wish I could fly.

   At least I could go after him.

   Try to find him.

   Just so see if he's OK.

***

*Night time. Lights up on **MAGNUS**, who is performing in Stornoway's hottest pole dancing club.*

Whoops of delight from his audience.

*Enter **HOPE**.*

She watches and doesn't watch.

He sees her leaving.

***

HOPE *and* **MAGNUS** *at the harbour.*

HOPE *looks at a newspaper headline.*

HOPE: 'Full Scale Emergency as Military Drone is Struck by Mysterious Large Bird over Stornoway.'

36

MAGNUS: It was totally the other way round. I was definitely struck by the military drone.

HOPE: Christ Magnus!

MAGNUS: It was disorientating coming down in Stornoway.

Peat smoke. Diesel. Thai green curry.

It was pure luck I came down in the harbour.

HOPE: You're lucky to be alive.

MAGNUS: I'm fine.

Pause.

HOPE: Can you not get a regular job?

…

Fantasy stripper?

MAGNUS: Pole dancer! I'm a pole dancer!

And it's cash in hand.

Well not always … exactly … in hand.

…

It's causing a bit of a sensation.

HOPE: I can imagine.

MAGNUS: Aw naw … they love it … the tourists are flocking in. But the Councillors can't agree what kind of licence we need. They can't decide if it's burlesque performance or a travelling circus with wild animals.

HOPE: What?

MAGNUS: Quote, any species not normally domesticated in Great Britain, unquote.

HOPE: You're probably more domesticated than they are!

MAGNUS: I don't think they're bothered that I cook lasagne.

HOPE: Well they should be.

MAGNUS: And we're having some issues with birdwatchers and their binoculars.

HOPE: … ?

MAGNUS: You know, you can … zoom in.

Pause.

HOPE: I am really not sure how I feel about pole dancing.

MAGNUS: Mum … you slept with a Swan.

HOPE: …

MAGNUS: Why don't you call into the club and I'll buy you a drink.

HOPE: I don't want to cramp your style.

MAGNUS: You can meet the others.

There's quite a few Fliers here.

Most of them are just passing through, but there's four of us renting a house in Ness.

There's Ingrid, she's part Pinkfoot, from Greenland.

Tito, Spoonbill, from Spain.

And then there's Dora. She says she's a Goldeneye from London but we're not convinced. She's a bit mad … I think she's maybe part Collie.

HOPE: Collie?!

MAGNUS: I'm kidding.

Anyway … it's a good laugh. Swing by the club and you can meet them.

HOPE: I don't know.

MAGNUS: I think you'll like them.

Pause.

HOPE: I was thinking. Maybe we should go on to Iceland, Magnus.

MAGNUS: Iceland? I heard it's all sky and water and it smells of eggs.

HOPE: And there's geysers, and waterfalls, and northern lights! We can swim in the hot springs.

MAGNUS: Visit the highland meadows of the central plateau?

HOPE: Maybe.

Beat.

MAGNUS: Mum, I've got something to tell you.

I probably should've told you before.

HOPE: …?

MAGNUS: I don't really like swans.

They're a bit … angry.

…

And they hiss.

Beat.

HOPE: They're not all like that, Magnus.

Pause.

HOPE: There's a boat leaving tomorrow.

MAGNUS: The forecast's not great.

HOPE: We could wait forever for the perfect day.

Where does that leave us?

Beat.

MAGNUS: You should go, Mum. But the troupe needs me. We're thinking of opening our own club. Flamenco-pole fusion.

HOPE: Does Stornoway need a Flamenco-pole fusion club?

MAGNUS: They do.

They just don't know it yet.

***

HOPE *alone. Shipping forecast.*

HOPE: Southeast Iceland. South-easterly five to seven perhaps gale eight later. Moderate or rough becoming rougher. Occasional rain, fog patches. Moderate or very poor.

A moment of decision.

HOPE: You could wait forever for the perfect day.

***

HOPE *in Iceland. She is in her element.*

PART 3

JOY is about to audition for 'So You Want to be a Midwife'. She breathes to calm herself. Nearby, her goldfish (Pedro Diecisiete) in a bowl. There is a lid on the bowl.

JOY: *(To self.)* Keep breathing.

Keep moving.

You're doing great.

Spotlight on **JOY**.

Hello?

…

Joy.

From Scotland.

…

Cause 'So You Want to Be a Midwife' is my favourite programme and cause I want to be a Midwife.

…

Loads of experience. Twenty years on a labour ward and ten in geriatric care.

…

Let's think … GCSE Spanish, Higher Anatomy Physiology and Health, O Grade Maths … SVQ 2 Cleaning and Support Services.

…

Si. Hablo Español … un poco.

…

Hobbies … eh …

Looks at the fish bowl.

Aquaculture.

...

A personal statement.

Beat.

I miss my mum.

...

Great! Yeah!

...

I mean, I'll have to check my schedule, but ... yeah.

***

JOY *and* **HOPE** *in the flat.*

JOY: I got your postcard. Iceland looks nice. Lots of birds.

HOPE: Iceland has fulmars. And loons. And shearwaters.

Oyster catchers, gannets, razorbills. Eider ducks, skuas, kittiwakes.

Iceland has puffins.

JOY: Aw ... did you visit the Highland Meadows? Still tracking him? Your graceful Icelandic lover.

HOPE: No! Of course not.

That battery died years ago.

But I went up to the nesting sites.

JOY: And ... ?

HOPE: And it's getting harder for them. We've been draining wetlands for years, but they support huge populations.

JOY: Whooper Swans?

HOPE: All of us really.

Pause.

HOPE: You got another goldfish.

JOY: This one keeps trying to jump out. He'll be the death of me.

Pedro Diecisiete thinks he's actually a flying fish. Yesterday I found him in my poke of chips.

JOY: *(To Pedro.)* No puedes volar, Pedro.

HOPE: Why does he speak Spanish?

JOY: Hope, he's a fish. He doesn't speak Spanish.

HOPE: Then why do you speak to him in Spanish?

JOY: My mum always spoke to the goldfish like that.

She was quite fluent.

I don't know how.

We never really talked about it.

HOPE: Never?

JOY: Ach … it was always difficult. Nowadays we'd be in relationship counselling or something.

But back then you didn't have relationships.

At least not with your mother.

A moment, shared.

JOY: How's Magnus?

***

MAGNUS *in Stornoway.*

Flamenco-Celtico pole fusion.

***

JOY *and* **HOPE** *in the flat. They are looking for Pedro, who has escaped his bowl.*

JOY: ¡Mierda!

¡Pedro!

Not again!

JOY *find him and puts him back in his bowl.*

PEDRO *is fine.* **JOY** *is gasping for breath.*

43

JOY: *(Pedro.)* You don't have wings!

Pause.

HOPE: Do you think he needs more space?

JOY: Space?

HOPE: Maybe he'd be happier in the pond.

JOY: He wouldn't survive a day out there.

HOPE: A day's probably quite a long time for a goldfish.

JOY: Why do people say that? It's a load of shite. They have a memory span of three months. They can see colours. They can feel sound. In the right conditions, they keep growing till they die.

HOPE: I really think he'd be better off outside.

JOY: He'd miss his treats.

HOPE: All the treats he'll need are in the pond.

Pause.

JOY: What about the other fish.

What if they don't like him?

HOPE: Of course they'll like him. He's so shiny!

Beat.

HOPE: You could let him adapt gradually. Put a wee drop pond water in his bowl every day. Let him get used to it.

Pause.

JOY: He might like that. Maybe it is time for a wee change.

***

HOPE *is practising delivering a lecture.*

HOPE: 'During the breeding season, environmental conditions in the Highland Meadows are critical to juvenile abundance and to the survival rates of hatchlings and fledglings.'

Beat.

HOPE: 'However, this new agricultural activity does not fully explain the changes in flight paths and behaviours.

Young birds in particular …'

Pause.

HOPE: 'Young birds in particular seem to be responding to environmental trends that humans are not yet aware of. This is clearly part of a bigger picture, in which all living organisms interconnect. One that is only illuminated when we consider the environment from the point of view of other species.'

Beat.

HOPE: 'We conclude that the ability to adapt is fundamental to the survival of any species. And radical changes in the environment demand revolutionary shifts in behaviour.'

Pause.

HOPE: Questions?

***

JOY *and* **HOPE** *at the bench with Pedro in his bowl.* **JOY** *has taken her shoes and socks off.*

A moment.

HOPE: Are you ready?

JOY: I'm not sure. I don't really know what I'm doing.

HOPE: None of us know what we're doing, Joy.

But most things aren't that complicated.

Beat.

JOY: Te quiero mucho Pedro. ¿Sabes?

JOY *takes a deep breath. She is walking into the water.*

This is harder than I thought.

…

Do you really think he'll be OK?

HOPE: He'll be fine.

JOY: It's quite cold. Is it too cold for him?

HOPE: He's cold-blooded.

JOY hesitates.

HOPE: Keep going.

Another step. **JOY** *is holding her breath.*

HOPE: And breathe.

JOY breathes.

HOPE: There.

…

Now keep moving.

…

Keep breathing.

…

You're doing great.

Flowing, rushing: air, water, blood.

***

MAGNUS *is in the club,* **HOPE** *is in Iceland,* **JOY** *is in the park.*

JOY: *(To Pedro.)* Keep moving. Keep breathing.

…

You're doing great.

Sound of a heartbeat decreases in frequency and increases in volume until it sounds like the beating wings of a large bird.

END

The Return

an Eden Court commission

The Return was first performed on Thursday 15 February 2018 in the OneTouch Theatre, Eden Court. This production then toured Scotland.

BERTRANDE	Emilie Patry
ARNAUD	Thoren Ferguson
SANXI	Greg Sinclair

Creative Team	
Director	Philip Howard
Designer	Kenneth MacLeod
Lighting and Sound Designer	Mike Savage
Movement Director	EJ Boyle
Composer	Greg Sinclair
Stage Manager	Sam Ramsay

Characters

Performer 1
BERTRANDE has been a single parent and head of her own household for seven years (since her husband walked out). She lives in the village where she was brought up.

Performer 2
ARNAUD arrives in the village from over the pass.

Performer 3
SANXI is **BERTRANDE**'s son. He appears as an adult and as a ten-year-old boy. This part is performed by a cellist.

A valley in the foothills of the French Pyrenees.
Circa 1560.

This is a valley that is home to: a river, vultures, crickets, owls, woodpeckers, chiff-chaffs, wild boar, trees that creak.

Act 1

Early September.

The home. There is a cello in the space. **SANXI** *enters. He picks up the cello and plays.*

Enter **ARNAUD**.

A moment.

ARNAUD: I'm sorry … I must've …

Are you alone?

SANXI: Do I know you?

ARNAUD: No. At least I don't think so. Sorry. I'm just …

I'm looking for work.

SANXI: You'd have to ask my mother.

ARNAUD: Is she here?

SANXI: She's up by the bridge … seeing to the sheep.

ARNAUD: Right.

And you are …

SANXI: Sanxi.

ARNAUD: Sanxi.

Yes.

…

Thank you.

ARNAUD *leaves.*

SCENE 2

A meadow.

BERTRANDE *is herding sheep and chasing off a vulture.*

At some point during this sequence, **ARNAUD** *enters and helps her. She doesn't see him.*

BERTRANDE: Shoo! Shoo!

…

Hup hup.

…

Hup hup … hup.

…

Shoo!

…

Hup hup.

…

Hup hup … hup.

…

Hup.

…

Shoo! Shoo!

…

Hup!

…

Hup hup.

….

Hup hup … hup.

…

Hup hup.

…

Hup hup hup.

…

Shoo!

Eventually the sheep are contained.

ARNAUD: That one won't be back in a hurry.

BERTRANDE *stops. She turns to look at him. They look at each other for a long moment.*

BERTRANDE: I wouldn't count on it.

The vultures are tenacious round here.

ARNAUD: Perhaps I should be more careful.

Perhaps I'll get carried off in my sleep.

BERTRANDE: You might.

The vulture is back.

BERTRANDE: Shoo!

ARNAUD: I don't suppose anyone would miss me.

BERTRANDE: Where have you come from?

ARNAUD: Over the pass.

BERTRANDE: And before that?

ARNAUD: Spain.

BERTRANDE: Spain.

ARNAUD: What brings you up here?

BERTRANDE: I live here! These are my sheep.

ARNAUD: It's not easy herding sheep on your own.

BERTRANDE: It's not. There's always one trying to escape.

She points to one of the sheep.

BERTRANDE: And it's always that one.

ARNAUD: Do they all belong to you?

BERTRANDE: *(Fast.)* Yan, tyan, tethera, methera, pimp, sethera, lethera, hovera, dovera, dik.

Sanadik, tyanadik, tetheradik, metheradik, bumfitt.

Not all of them. There's one slipped in.

That one isn't mine.

From over the pass by the looks of it.

ARNAUD: How can you tell?

BERTRANDE: It just has that look about it. It's different around the face. They're prettier on the other side. Our sheep are quite ugly.

ARNAUD: I think they're exotic. With their square jaws and long legs.

BERTRANDE: They're really quite ugly.

BERTRANDE *looks over her sheep.*

ARNAUD: What will you do with the imposter?

BERTRANDE: Maybe next spring I'll take it back over the pass.

Or maybe not. There's plenty of mine go the other way. Anyway, it's good for the stock.

The breeding.

ARNAUD: That one's got footrot.

That'll be why the vulture was hanging about.

BERTRANDE: What do you know about it?

ARNAUD: They might look different, but sheep are sheep.

Have you put tarantula venom on it?

BERTRANDE: We don't have that many tarantulas running about here.

I'll take it back down with me. Put it in the barn for a bit. Cut out the maggots.

ARNAUD: Have you a big barn?

BERTRANDE: Big enough.

ARNAUD: What about the others?

BERTRANDE: I'll let them back out. They don't go far. I'll put a block of salt by the pen.

ARNAUD takes two apples from his pocket and offers one to BERTRANDE.

She takes it and looks at it. It's not a type of apple she has seen before.

BERTRANDE: That's an exotic looking apple.

ARNAUD: It's a Spanish apple.

ARNAUD takes big bites from his apple.

BERTRANDE: Is that how they eat their apples in Spain?

ARNAUD: This is the way I eat my apples.

BERTRANDE takes out her knife, cleans it and slices her apple. ARNAUD watches her. BERTRANDE notices him watching.

BERTRANDE: This is how we eat our apples here.

She eats.

BERTRANDE: So what brings you here?

ARNAUD: I'm looking for work.

BERTRANDE: What can you do?

ARNAUD: I can turn my hand to most things. If I had a roof over my head I could help out around the village.

…

Do you think someone would take me on?

BERTRANDE: I don't know. They're suspicious of outsiders.

Taking their women.

Or worse, their sheep.

Pause.

BERTRANDE: I should get back down to the village.

ARNAUD: Is there someone waiting for you?

BERTRANDE: My son.

I have a son.

ARNAUD: Yes.

BERTRANDE: I should get back to my son.

ARNAUD: I'll guard the troop for you.

    See that they don't wander off.

BERTRANDE: And how do I know you won't steal them?

ARNAUD: You don't. You'll just have to take a chance.

BERTRANDE: Will you be staying long?

ARNAUD: Perhaps I'll stay till the snow comes.

BERTRANDE: It might not be far off.

ARNAUD: There was frost on my blanket this morning.

BERTRANDE: Where are you sleeping?

ARNAUD: A cave on the hillside.

BERTRANDE: You'll be cold right enough.

ARNAUD: I'm used to it

SCENE 3

Four days later. **SANXI** *is at home.*

BERTRANDE *enters. She starts kneading dough.*

SANXI: Tell me about the day I was born.

BERTRANDE: Sanxi! Again?

SANXI: Where was my father that day?

BERTRANDE: Where was he?

SANXI: What was he doing?

    Pause.

BERTRANDE: He was chopping wood. He was chopping wood and the axe slipped on a knot. We bound it with his shirt. I never could get the blood out. It was a waste of a good shirt.

SANXI: Tell me more.

BERTRANDE: I've told you it all before.

SANXI: Tell me something else.

BERTRANDE: Have you heard the story about the shepherdess and the bear?

SANXI: The one where she gets eaten by the bear?

BERTRANDE: The one where he takes her to his cave in the woods and rolls a boulder across the entrance.

SANXI: Yes. I've heard it.

BERTRANDE: Every day, the bear goes out for food. And every day he brings her back a gift … daisies / honey

SANXI: Yeah yeah. I know.

She's intrigued by his kindness, his strong, hairy arms, and the way he nuzzles her neck. Blah. Blah. Blah.

…

I'd like to kill a bear. I'd need a bigger knife though, to kill a bear.

Could I get a bigger knife do you think?

BERTRANDE: You're not going to kill a bear.

SANXI: Why not?

BERTRANDE: You're ten!

SANXI: Well a boar maybe.

BERTRANDE: Maybe a squirrel.

SANXI: I've already caught dozens of squirrels.

BERTRANDE: Or a hare?

SANXI: Will you take me hunting?

BERTRANDE: I don't have time to take you hunting.

SANXI: Père Raymond says he'll take me hunting.

  BERTRANDE *stops what she's doing.*

BERTRANDE: I'll take you hunting.

SANXI: When?

BERTRANDE: Soon.

SANXI: You always say that. Soon when?

BERTRANDE: When I have time.

SANXI: You never have time.

BERTRANDE wipes her hands.

BERTRANDE: Maybe if you helped out?

SANXI: Maybe if you didn't have to look after the sheep.

Pause.

BERTRANDE: Take this bread down to the oven Sanxi.

SANXI: That's women's work.

BERTRANDE: It's up to you.

You want to eat bread you take it down to the oven.

BERTRANDE leaves.

SCENE 4

BERTRANDE *is just downstream of the bridge, wiping a knife on a cloth.*

Enter **ARNAUD**.

ARNAUD: You're back.

BERTRANDE: I thought I should check on the sheep. See that they hadn't wandered over the pass. See that they hadn't been stolen.

ARNAUD: And the knife?

BERTRANDE: Trimming their hooves.

ARNAUD: I'll help.

BERTRANDE: I'm done.

She wipes the knife.

BERTRANDE: I thought you'd left already, but then I saw you were keeping the fire going.

ARNAUD: I went to gather myrtles.

BERTRANDE: Myrtles?

ARNAUD: Here …

He offers her some.

BERTRANDE: Blaeberries.

ARNAUD: Blaeberries.

BERTRANDE: That's what we call them here.

ARNAUD: If I wanted to fit in here I'd have to use your words for things.

BERTRANDE: If you wanted to fit in here, you'd have to cut your apples.

ARNAUD: That might be difficult.

BERTRANDE: Hard.

ARNAUD: See.

It's difficult / already

BERTRANDE: Hard.

ARNAUD: Hard …. already.

Fitting in.

BERTRANDE: I know.

Pause.

BERTRANDE: Has anyone else been up here?

ARNAUD: I've only seen you.

No one else knows I'm here

BERTRANDE: Apart from the sheep.

ARNAUD: Will you stop here and eat with me?

BERTRANDE: I will.

ARNAUD: I should catch some fish then.

BERTRANDE: You invite me for lunch and you haven't even caught it yet?

ARNAUD: You won't have to wait long.

BERTRANDE: I won't have to wait long. I'll catch my own!

ARNAUD: Fair enough.

You probably know the best tickling pools.

BERTRANDE: Tickling pools?

ARNAUD: You know … *(He mimes guddling for fish.)*

61

BERTRANDE: Guddling pools.

ARNAUD: Guddling pools.

Of course.

I probably sound strange.

BERTRANDE: I like the way you speak.

It's interesting.

It's exotic.

ARNAUD: It's just the novelty of it. It's like ugly sheep. You would soon tire of it.

BERTRANDE: You go first … I'll let you have the first one.

He guddles, catches one, but it escapes.

ARNAUD: Slippery buggers.

BERTRANDE: Let me show you.

The fish round here need a firm grip.

Like this …

BERTRANDE *traps* **ARNAUD**'s *hand as if it were a fish.*

BERTRANDE: You have warm hands.

ARNAUD: Or you have cold hands.

BERTRANDE: Sorry.

ARNAUD: No. I like the feel of your cold hands.

BERTRANDE: Good.

Pause.

BERTRANDE: So can I touch you here?

Wrist.

ARNAUD: …

BERTRANDE: And here?

Shoulder.

ARNAUD: Yes.

BERTRANDE: And here?

Cheek.

BERTRANDE: What did they call you?

In Spain?

ARNAUD: Arno.

BERTRANDE: Arnaud.

Nice.

Exotic.

ARNAUD: Are you still hungry?

BERTRANDE: Ravenous.

ARNAUD: I would like to eat with you.

BERTRANDE: I would like to eat with you.

ARNAUD: I think I would like to eat with you often.

BERTRANDE: It's not seemly for a married woman to eat with another man.

Pause.

ARNAUD: I don't suppose your husband would be too pleased.

Pause.

BERTRANDE: My husband's away.

ARNAUD: Shepherd?

BERTRANDE: No.

ARNAUD: Merchant?

BERTRANDE *shrugs.*

ARNAUD: Mercenary.

BERTRANDE: I don't know.

He just left.

He's been away for seven years.

ARNAUD: Perhaps he'll come back then.

BERTRANDE: I doubt it.

ARNAUD: Do you miss him?

BERTRANDE: I don't know.

...

I don't know if I miss him.

ARNAUD: Some places, you can divorce an absent husband.

BERTRANDE: I heard that.

But not here.

ARNAUD: It will come here too.

BERTRANDE: I don't know what difference it'll make. You can change the laws but people don't change.

Pause.

ARNAUD: Were you happy?

BERTRANDE: Happy?

ARNAUD: Were you happy when you married?

BERTRANDE: I was twelve.

ARNAUD: And he was ....

BERTRANDE: Shy.

...

We didn't have a child. Not at first.

...

Not for a long time.

They said we were bewitched.

Eventually Père Raymond said four masses and had us eat holy wafers baked in the hearth. And then Sanxi was born. Named after Martin's father.

ARNAUD: Martin liked his father?

BERTRANDE: They quarrelled.

ARNAUD: Sons quarrel with their fathers.

BERTRANDE: They were too similar.

Sons resemble their fathers. That's why he left.

ARNAUD: Is it?

BERTRANDE: He left because he stole some grain from his father.

ARNAUD: I can't imagine/ him

BERTRANDE: He stole some grain from his father.

ARNAUD: You're sure about/ that?

BERTRANDE: Yes.

Pause.

ARNAUD: And after that?

BERTRANDE: I don't know.

ARNAUD: Perhaps he became a pedlar.

BERTRANDE: Or a shepherd.

ARNAUD: Perhaps he went to fight for the Spanish.

A footsoldier for Felipe Dos.

Pause.

BERTRANDE: You've been to Spain.

Tell me something about Spain.

ARNAUD: What kind of thing?

BERTRANDE: Any thing.

ARNAUD: The women / wear

BERTRANDE: Tell me about bears. Tell me about bears in Spain.

ARNAUD: In the green mountains of Spain there's a woman who is half
bear.

BERTRANDE: Have you seen her?

ARNAUD: I caught a glimpse of her once. When I was picking …
blaeberries.

BERTRANDE: What does she look like?

ARNAUD: She has nails like claws, and wide, short feet. She has a round body and hairy limbs. She has curly, tangled hair, lips like a muzzle, a flat nose and bright, bright eyes.

BERTRANDE: And how was she born?

ARNAUD: They say her mother was a woman and her father, a bear.

BERTRANDE: Is she strong?

ARNAUD: She can carry a horse round her neck.

She can lift boulders from mountain streams.

She can break a tree trunk with her bare hands.

BERTRANDE: Bear hands.

BERTRANDE *gets out some bread and honey.*

BERTRANDE: I like your stories.

They eat.

ARNAUD: This honey …

BERTRANDE: Don't you like it?

ARNAUD: You don't get honey like this anywhere else.

Pause.

ARNAUD: There was a flurry of snow last night.

BERTRANDE: If you wanted somewhere warm to sleep …

ARNAUD: Yes?

BERTRANDE: My barn is big enough.

SCENE 5

BERTRANDE *sings a song about new love.*

SONG: Nouvele Amor Qui Si M'Agree *(Rogeret de Cambrai)*

Nouvele amor qui si m'agree

De joli cuer mi fait chanter,

Et cele ou j'ai mis ma pensee

Me tient en bone volenté.

Sans demoree

Li ai donee

M'amor, ja ne l'en quier oster;

Ja n'iert fausee

Mes melz amee,

Se de cuer mi voloit amer.

Por li fas soner ma vïele

Tant doucement et main et soir

D'un douz penser que me resveille

Des biens que je soloie avoir.

Cortoise et sage,

Et cler visage,

Onc de mes euz plus bele ne vi.

Se vostre amor

Ne m'assoage,

Je ne vos quier metre en oubli.

A moment.

BERTRANDE *and* **ARNAUD** *have just made love.*

BERTRANDE: What do you see?

ARNAUD: Where?

BERTRANDE: In the grain of the wood.

ARNAUD: A battlefield.

...

What do you see?

BERTRANDE: Two lovers, dancing.

Pause.

ARNAUD: Did you joy?

BERTRANDE: Did I joy?

ARNAUD: You know …

Did you … *(**ARNAUD** groans as if he's having an orgasm.)*

BERTRANDE: We don't call it 'joying' here.

ARNAUD: What do you call it?

BERTRANDE: I don't think we have a word for it.

We don't talk about it much.

ARNAUD: But did you?

BERTRANDE: Well no. When I *(**BERTRANDE** groans as if she's having an orgasm)* I actually *(Really shouts like she's really having an orgasm.)*

ARNAUD: Did you not like it then?

BERTRANDE: Of course I liked it.

I loved it when you …

BERTRANDE *sticks her tongue out and licks suggestively.*

ARNAUD: It was pleasing?

BERTRANDE: It was different.

ARNAUD: Did your husband not lick the honeypot?

BERTRANDE: … ?

ARNAUD: …

BERTRANDE: No.

No he didn't.

ARNAUD: Maybe I shouldn't do it then.

BERTRANDE: But I liked it.

ARNAUD: But you didn't joy.

BERTRANDE: Not yet.

…

Where did you learn to lick the honeypot?

ARNAUD: You know.

BERTRANDE: No, I don't know.

ARNAUD: Books.

BERTRANDE: … ?

ARNAUD: You must have books.

BERTRANDE: I've seen books.

But not books like that.

ARNAUD: I can show you again if you like?

BERTRANDE: Maybe later.

…

If you're staying.

ARNAUD: I would stay if you wanted me to.

But I would be more help to you if you'd let me into the house.

BERTRANDE: Don't you like my barn?

ARNAUD: I'm not much use to you when I'm stuck in the barn.

BERTRANDE: You have your uses.

ARNAUD: Even that would be better somewhere else.

BERTRANDE picks hay off him.

ARNAUD: Take me into your bed.

BERTRANDE: I don't know. You might not want to leave.

ARNAUD: Would that be so bad?

BERTRANDE: They wouldn't look kindly on it in the village.

I'm a married woman.

ARNAUD: I think they would forgive you.

After all this time.

BERTRANDE: People have long memories here.

Pause.

ARNAUD: What if I actually was your husband. Returned from his travels.

…

But a better man.

BERTRANDE: A better man?

ARNAUD: Yes.

…

I could pretend to be Martin.

BERTRANDE *inspects him.*

BERTRANDE: You have the same hair.

The same teeth.

The same scars.

The same …

…

Well … not quite the same.

But quite pleasing.

Pause.

ARNAUD: Pleasing?

BERTRANDE: I think we could get away with it.

ARNAUD: Live as man and wife?

BERTRANDE: Or as woman and husband.

BERTRANDE *takes a crystal from round her neck.*

ARNAUD: I wasn't asking you to marry me.

BERTRANDE: I know.

I'm asking you.

She hangs the crystal round his neck.

BERTRANDE: We'll drink to it.

BERTRANDE *offers him a drink from a gourd.*

BERTRANDE: Apple brandy.

A moment.

ARNAUD: I don't drink spirits.

BERTRANDE: You used to.

ARNAUD: A drinker?

BERTRANDE: You don't have to.

Maybe you've stopped.

ARNAUD: No, I should.

I will.

He takes the gourd.

She takes it back.

BERTRANDE: No. Don't.

I'd feel bad if you started and you couldn't stop.

Or if you drank too much and had an accident.

I'd be a widow.

ARNAUD: Yes.

BERTRANDE *takes a drink from the gourd. And another.*

BERTRANDE: Your lovers will be pleased you're back.

ARNAUD: Lovers?

BERTRANDE: There were a few.

ARNAUD: How many?

BERTRANDE: Rose, for example.

ARNAUD: Rose?

BERTRANDE: Rose.

ARNAUD: What's she like?

BERTRANDE: *(As Rose.)* 'Ma tits urnae just headin tae the sea Hen, thur's wan gaun tae the Atlantic and wan tae the Med.'

ARNAUD: She sounds charming.

BERTRANDE: She's my best friend.

ARNAUD: Oh.

BERTRANDE: And maybe also …

…

Never mind.

ARNAUD: I think I should know.

BERTRANDE: Père Raymond, the Priest.

ARNAUD: The Priest?

BERTRANDE: *(As Père Raymond.)* Well who can blame you? He's very …

Pause.

ARNAUD: I'm sorry.

BERTRANDE: What for?

Pause.

ARNAUD: I don't know.

For cheating.

For leaving.

…

I've changed.

BERTRANDE: I know.

You're a different man.

ARNAUD: But I'm still your husband?

BERTRANDE: If you want to be.

ARNAUD: I can be whoever you want me to be.

BERTRANDE: You're Martin.

Martin Guerre has returned.

We have to believe that.

We have to believe it or no one else will.

ARNAUD: The return of Martin Guerre.

BERTRANDE: You're back.

ARNAUD: I'm back.

72

SCENE 6

Next morning. **SANXI**, **ARNAUD** *and* **BERTRANDE** *in the house.* **BERTRANDE** *crosses bread with a knife, then cuts it.* **SANXI** *doesn't look at* **ARNAUD**.

BERTRANDE: Come and eat with us Sanxi.

Pause.

The cello speaks **SANXI**'s *lines.*

ARNAUD: I'll wipe your face.

SANXI: It doesn't need wiped.

BERTRANDE: Do as your father says.

SANXI: *(To* **BERTRANDE**.*)* My face doesn't need wiped.

Maybe your face needs wiped.

Maybe your eyes need washed.

Maybe your ears need cleaned out.

BERTRANDE: Sanxi. Your father is back.

SANXI: From where?

BERTRANDE: From over the pass.

SANXI: Hundreds of people come over the pass. They're trying to escape the fighting. They're trying to get over before the snow comes. They're hiding in the hills and stealing the sheep.

BERTRANDE: He's your father because I say he's your father.

SANXI: He's not my father.

BERTRANDE: *(To* **ARNAUD**.*)* He'll get used to it.

SANXI: I won't.

BERTRANDE: You'll have to.

SANXI: He'll have to prove it. He'll have to prove he's my father.

BERTRANDE: Sanxi!

ARNAUD: No. He's right. I'll prove it. I'll prove I'm his father.

Pause.

BERTRANDE: *(To* **ARNAUD**.*)* There's a dance tonight.

ARNAUD: …

BERTRANDE: We should all go.

ARNAUD: Do I have to?

> **SANXI** *looks at* **ARNAUD** *for the first time.*

BERTRANDE: If you want to fit in, you have to go to the dance.

ARNAUD: We'll all go.

BERTRANDE: We should practise.

> **BERTRANDE** *demonstrates a Fandango.*

ARNAUD: Or maybe not.

BERTRANDE: It's not so hard.

Look.

She teaches him the Fandango.

They dance. He's a good dancer. It's as if he has been dancing this all his life.

BERTRANDE: You're a good dancer.

ARNAUD: I always was a good dancer.

BERTRANDE: We'll see.

SCENE 7

The village dance. (Branle, Rondeau, Fandango.)

Dancing.

ARNAUD: *(As the tailor.)* 'Ye'll be aifter a new jaicket Martin, noo yer back.

Funny but … yer taller than Ah remember.

Mibbe just loast a bit ae weight, eh?'

Dancing.

BERTRANDE: *(As Rose.)* 'Zat you Martin? My goad. It's been a while.

Is it really you but?

Tell ye whit.

Prove it.

Shoaz yer bum.'

Dancing

ARNAUD: *(As Père Raymond.)* 'Of course, it's not merely a matter of husbandry Martin, but a union of spirits. You will, I trust, take your responsibilities seriously?'

Dancing.

BERTRANDE: *(As an older woman.)* Oor Martin wis aye licht oan his feet. A bonnie dancer an' a richt guid fechter.

Dancing.

ARNAUD: *(As the tailor.)* 'Ye can pay me in the Spring Martin. Wance ye see whit lambs ye've goat.'

Dancing.

BERTRANDE: *(As Rose.)* 'Aye. It's him all right! Ah'd ken that bum anywhere.'

Dancing (Fandango).

ARNAUD *plays a Spanish tune on his fiddle.*

BERTRANDE *takes him outside. They breathe in the fresh air.*

ARNAUD: How am I doing?

BERTRANDE: Not bad.

But you need to be careful.

ARNAUD: No more Spanish tunes.

Pause.

BERTRANDE: Martin was born in the Basque country. There were certain words he always used from his mother tongue.

ARNAUD: Like?

BERTRANDE: Ama.

ARNAUD: Ama?

BERTRANDE: Mother.

ARNAUD: Anything else?

BERTRANDE: Txakur.

ARNAUD: Txakur?

BERTRANDE: Dog.

ARNAUD: Txakur.

BERTRANDE: And Seme.

ARNAUD: Seme?

BERTRANDE: Son.

And Putaseme

ARNAUD: Son of a … ?

BERTRANDE: Yes.

ARNAUD: Anything else I should know?

BERTRANDE: He was quite acrobatic.

Raised eyebrows.

BERTRANDE: He could do cartwheels.

ARNAUD *does a cartwheel.*

BERTRANDE: And handstands.

ARNAUD *does a handstand.*

BERTRANDE: And somersaults.

ARNAUD: Putaseme!

BERTRANDE: I'm joking.

…

Right … again.

ARNAUD: Fandango?

BERTRANDE: Honeypot.

SCENE 8

They sing as they work.

Diga, Janeta,

Te vos-ti louga, Larireto!

Diga, Janeta,

Te vos-ti louga?

Nani, ma mairo,

Me vole marida, Larireto!

Nani, ma mairo,

Me vole marida.

SCENE 9

Mid September.

ARNAUD *is tramping grapes.*

ARNAUD: Have you heard the one about the shepherdess and the bear?

SANXI: The one where he takes her to his cave and rolls a boulder across
the entrance?

ARNAUD: The one where she lures the bear with an injured sheep,
captures him and enslaves him.

And every day, she sends him out to bring back gifts … daisies,
raspberries …

Until one day he returns weary, tells her he's tired of the pretence and
takes off his bear coat, revealing the nearly hairless body of … a man.

SANXI: That's not the way I heard it.

ARNAUD: No?

SANXI: I heard she picked up a stone and hit him right between the eyes,
bringing him crashing down with a thud.

ARNAUD: Ouf!

SANXI: Then she plunged her knife into his heart and dissected him very
carefully, so that nothing was wasted. She made a rug, a saddle and
a tunic with his skin, needles with his teeth and tools from his bones.
And she ate bear meat all winter … boiled, roasted, salted, dried,
smoked … even though it wasn't her favourite.

Pause.

ARNAUD: I never heard that one before.

ARNAUD *stops tramping.*

ARNAUD: These grapes came from your vine.

SANXI: My vine?

ARNAUD: The vine that I planted for you when you were born.

SANXI: Where were you the day I was born?

ARNAUD *tramps.*

ARNAUD: The day you were born I was cutting hay and when I heard your mother's cries I cut my leg with the scythe.

SANXI: A scythe?

ARNAUD: That one.

SANXI: You have hundreds of scars.

Pause.

SANXI: Was it a bad cut?

ARNAUD: I ripped a sheet to bind it.

SANXI: Not a shirt?

ARNAUD: Why would I ruin a shirt?

SANXI: Why did you leave?

ARNAUD *stops tramping.*

ARNAUD: An argument.

Grown-up stuff.

Boring stuff.

ARNAUD *steps out of the barrel.*

SANXI *washes* **ARNAUD**'s *feet.*

ARNAUD: Tell me a joke.

SANXI: Knock knock.

ARNAUD: Who's there?

SANXI: Cows go.

ARNAUD: Cows go who?

SANXI: Cows go moo not who.

ARNAUD: Knock knock.

SANXI: Who's there?

ARNAUD: Ivan.

SANXI: Ivan who?

ARNAUD: I vant to come in.

SANXI: Knock knock.

ARNAUD: Who's there?

SANXI: Adore.

ARNAUD: Adore who?

SANXI: Adore is between us.

ARNAUD: Knock knock.

SANXI: Who's there?

ARNAUD: Annie.

SANXI: Annie who?

ARNAUD: Anyone you like.

SANXI: Do you think you would always know me?

ARNAUD: What do you mean?

SANXI: If I went away … for a few years say. Then came back.

Would you recognise me?

ARNAUD: Of course I would.

SCENE 10

October.

ARNAUD *and* **BERTRANDE** *are on opposite sides of the valley. These are the words they whistle.*

ARNAUD: Up here.

BERTRANDE: Injured?

ARNAUD: Lame.

BERTRANDE: Bring her down.

ARNAUD: Meet me at the bridge.

BERTRANDE: What for?

ARNAUD: Tickling.

BERTRANDE: Guddling.

ARNAUD: Meet me at the bridge.

SCENE 11

November.

BERTRANDE *whistles the tune for 'Nouvele amor qui si m'agree' as she peels apples.*
ARNAUD *sharpens a knife.*

SANXI *is upset and shivering.*

BERTRANDE: What's wrong?

SANXI: It doesn't matter.

BERTRANDE: Of course it matters.

SANXI: They took my knife.

BERTRANDE: Who did?

SANXI: The same boys as always.

ARNAUD: You should leather them.

BERTRANDE: He will not!

ARNAUD: In Toulouse you would lose an ear for stealing a knife.

BERTRANDE: They're just boys.

ARNAUD: Why do you think they pick on him? They pick on him because he doesn't fight back.

BERTRANDE: Nonsense. It's probably because he's small.

SANXI: *(To **BERTRANDE**)* It's probably because you're sleeping with a foreigner! It's probably because you're lying and fucking like a bitch on heat.

ARNAUD *is about to strike* **SANXI**. **BERTRANDE** *stops him.*

BERTRANDE: Don't you ever lift a hand to my Son!

ARNAUD: I can't let him speak to you like that!

BERTRANDE: You can't tell him what to do.

ARNAUD: Didn't you hear him? If the children are saying I'm not Martin then they're hearing it from somewhere

I have to prove I'm Martin.

I'm his father.

A father tells his son what to do.

A moment.

BERTRANDE *goes back to peeling the apples. She peels in strips from the top down.*

A moment, then **ARNAUD** *helps her. He peels in spirals.*

BERTRANDE: That's not the way we do it here.

Look …

She demonstrates.

ARNAUD: I think my way is better. There's a flow to it.

BERTRANDE: It doesn't matter if it's better. You have to do it our way if you're going to fit in.

ARNAUD: I have to peel apples your way?

BERTRANDE: It's not my way … it's our way. It's the way that we've always done it here.

ARNAUD: I don't know if I can do that.

BERTRANDE: It's easy! Look!

ARNAUD: That's not what I mean.

I mean … what if I don't want to change the way I peel apples?

BERTRANDE: Then they'll think … by the way you peel your apples … that you're not from here.

ARNAUD *puts down his knife and takes an apple. He is about to take a bite out of it.*

BERTRANDE: And by the way you eat your apples.

ARNAUD *picks up his knife and starts to slice his apple.*

A moment.

SANXI: Did you hear the one about the shepherdess and the bear?

ARNAUD: The one where she cuts him up and eats him?

BERTRANDE: Cuts him up and eats him?

SANXI: No. The one where she sends him out to bring back gifts … flowers, raspberries, honey …

Until one day he returns, tells her he's tired of pretending and takes off his bear coat, revealing the body of … a wolf.

ARNAUD: That's not the way I heard it.

SANXI: No?

ARNAUD: In the one I heard she traps him, takes him home and trains him to dance.

ARNAUD dances like a bear.

SANXI: I'd like to trap a bear.

ARNAUD: A boy is no match for a bear.

SANXI: A boar then.

ARNAUD: I'll take you hunting.

I'll take you hunting for wild boar.

ARNAUD puts a boar skin over his head.

ARNAUD: *(To SANXI.)* Hunt the boar!

BERTRANDE: He's not going to kill a boar!

ARNAUD: Why not?

BERTRANDE: He's too small.

ARNAUD: Small is good. Mostly you need stealth. To move quietly over cones and branches. Not to tread on mushrooms. To be odourless.

SANXI: I'd like to go hunting.

ARNAUD: We'll wait till the snow comes. It's easier to bring the boar down in the snow. The weight of them.

SANXI *takes an apple and bites into it as* **ARNAUD** *would.* **BERTRANDE** *watches him.* **SANXI** *notices her watching.*

SANXI: What are you looking at me like that for?

BERTRANDE: *(To* **ARNAUD**.*)* He's starting to look like you.

How is that possible?

ARNAUD: He's my son.

Sons resemble their fathers.

SCENE 12

Winter. It snows.

La fête de l'ours.

Act 2

SCENE 1

A boar hunt. The sound of wild boar in the undergrowth.

Then squealing

In the kitchen, **BERTRANDE** *is chopping herbs.*

SANXI: He grabbed it by the back legs and slashed the tendons so it couldn't get away and then boum … he got his knife right under the leg and up into its heart.

BERTRANDE *is nauseous.*

SANXI: Then he cut its throat and let the blood out and we hung it from a tree … the big oak tree by the bottom path … we hung it by its neck and snip cut it open and took its stomach out.

BERTRANDE *takes a handful of thyme and inhales it deeply.*

SANXI: Then we washed it out with water from the river and turned it over and hung it by its feet. It's easier to skin if it's hanging by its feet. You just pull the skin over its head like a jersey. Like a rabbit. But bigger.

ARNAUD: We'll get a big fire built tonight and put it on a spit. We'll invite the whole village.

BERTRANDE: Maybe we should smoke it. We might need it this Winter.

ARNAUD *tousles* **SANXI**'s *hair.*

ARNAUD: Fetch my boots, Bertrande.

BERTRANDE: Rose is away.

ARNAUD: I'm going to see Père Raymond.

BERTRANDE: Raymond?

ARNAUD: To ask him for the money.

BERTRANDE: What money?

ARNAUD: The money that he made renting out the orchard while I was away.

BERTRANDE: You can't ask for the rent back. It's not the way things are done round here.

ARNAUD: So?

BERTRANDE: You'll bring trouble.

ARNAUD: From the Priest?

BERTRANDE: You walked out and we never heard from you.

For all we knew you were dead.

ARNAUD: Well I'm back. And I'm a changed man.

We'll use the money to commission an apple press. We could make more cider with a press.

BERTRANDE: I don't think we need more cider.

ARNAUD: Rose says there's a future in cider.

BERTRANDE: Rose says a lot of things.

Rose says you can stave off morning sickness with a handful of thyme.

ARNAUD looks at her.

ARNAUD: Another child?

A moment.

ARNAUD: That didn't take long.

BERTRANDE: Maybe I'm just weary.

ARNAUD: No holy wafers this time.

She holds the thyme to her mouth and nose and inhales deeply again. ARNAUD watches her. SANXI watches her.

BERTRANDE sits.

ARNAUD: *(To SANXI.)* What do you think Sanxi, a baby brother?

BERTRANDE: Or sister.

Maybe.

It's early.

ARNAUD: A girl?

...

A girl would need a dowry.

ARNAUD *starts putting on his boots.*

BERTRANDE: Where are you going?

ARNAUD: I'm going to see Père Raymond.

I'll tell him you're pregnant and we need the money from the orchard.

BERTRANDE: Don't go.

ARNAUD: Why not?

BERTRANDE: I need help with the boar.

ARNAUD: I'll help you when I get back.

BERTRANDE: Please don't go to Père Raymond. You'll ruin everything.

ARNAUD: What do you mean?

BERTRANDE: We don't need the money. He'll resent you asking for the money. We shouldn't be greedy. We'll manage.

ARNAUD: I'm only asking for what's mine.

BERTRANDE: Yours?

ARNAUD: What?

BERTRANDE: It's ours.

ARNAUD: Mine. Ours. A word! What is it with women and words?

Pause.

BERTRANDE: What did you know about my affairs before we met in the meadow?

ARNAUD: I knew nothing.

How could I?

BERTRANDE: Did you know I had fourteen sheep? Did you know I had a barn?

...

Is that why you came back?

ARNAUD: Of course not.

ARNAUD *leaves.*

A moment.

BERTRANDE *goes back to chopping apples and herbs. She's distracted.*

BERTRANDE: *(To* **SANXI**.*)* We should wash the intestine. We should make the sausage before it goes off.

SANXI: We washed it already.

BERTRANDE: I'll chop the herbs but I can't face the innards.

SANXI: They say the heart of a pig is just like the heart of a man. That you could swap them and no one would know the difference.

BERTRANDE: I don't know if I've ever seen the heart of a man.

SANXI: Can I have the tongue?

BERTRANDE: All of it?

SANXI: It was quite a small boar.

A male, but small.

BERTRANDE: You want tongue, you cook it yourself.

BERTRANDE *goes out for air.*

SCENE 2

In the yard outside the house. **BERTRANDE** *is seated.*

ARNAUD *enters.*

A moment.

ARNAUD: He won't give me the money.

BERTRANDE: Of course he won't give you the money. He's a Priest. It's like getting milk from a fish.

ARNAUD: He won't give me the money because he doesn't believe I'm Martin.

BERTRANDE: He'll come round. Stop asking him for money and it'll blow over. He always said my house needs a man in it.

ARNAUD: He says I'm not Martin.

87

BERTRANDE: He can say what he likes.

ARNAUD: He says that I can't be Martin.

BERTRANDE: He doesn't want you to be Martin. He doesn't want you claiming the money he owes you. But if you just keep your head down/ for a bit we can…

ARNAUD: He says that I can't be Martin because you're pregnant.

BERTRANDE: …

ARNAUD: He says that I can't be Martin because you're pregnant.

He says that Martin never fathered a child.

BERTRANDE: …

ARNAUD: Is that true?

> **BERTRANDE** *says nothing but it's clear that it's true.*

ARNAUD: How could he know that?

BERTRANDE: …

ARNAUD: How could he know that!

Pause.

BERTRANDE: There's so much shame about not having a baby.

I thought it would be better for both of us.

ARNAUD: Four masses, holy wafers and cake, you said.

BERTRANDE: That too.

ARNAUD: You slept with the Priest.

Why would you do that?

BERTRANDE: Yes. Why would you do that?

Pause.

ARNAUD: Sanxi is not my son.

…

Is that why I left?

BERTRANDE: I don't know why you left.

You didn't tell me you were leaving.

You didn't tell anyone you were leaving.

Pause.

ARNAUD: And this baby?

BERTRANDE: Yours.

ARNAUD: Mine. You're sure of that?

BERTRANDE: It happens.

Pause.

ARNAUD: I don't know what to do.

BERTRANDE: Do nothing. Père Raymond won't want it getting out that he's Sanxi's father. Forget about the money from the orchard and do nothing.

ARNAUD: What would Martin have done? If he found out his wife had slept with the Priest.

BERTRANDE: I don't know.

ARNAUD *stands to leave.*

BERTRANDE: Where are you going?

He's leaving.

BERTRANDE: Where are you going!

SCENE 3

The next day.

BERTRANDE *alone. Outdoors.*

BERTRANDE: *(Shouts.)* Come and eat.

No response.

BERTRANDE: *(Whistled.)* Come and eat.

No response.

BERTRANDE: *(Whistled.)* Come down.

No response.

BERTRANDE: *(Spoken.)* Putaseme.

SCENE 4

BERTRANDE and **SANXI** *at home.*

SANXI: Will you remember me tomorrow?

BERTRANDE: Of course I'll remember you tomorrow.

SANXI: Will you remember me in one week?

BERTRANDE: What kind of question is that?

SANXI: Will you remember me in one month?

BERTRANDE: Yes Sanxi, I'll remember you in a month.

SANXI: Will you remember me in a year?

BERTRANDE: Stop pestering me!

SANXI: Knock knock.

BERTRANDE: Who's there?

SANXI: See. You've forgotten me already.

BERTRANDE: Knock knock.

SANXI: Who's there?

BERTRANDE: Wooden shoe.

SANXI: Wooden shoe who?

BERTRANDE: Wooden shoe like to hear a different joke?

SANXI: Very funny.

A moment.

BERTRANDE: Sanxi, can you smell something?

SANXI: The fire pit?

BERTRANDE: It's not that.

Something else is burning.

SANXI: The hair of the boar?

She smells the air again.

Bells.

BERTRANDE: It's burning hay.

...

SANXI: ... grab a bucket!

The Priest's barn burns to the ground despite their best efforts.

SCENE 5

BERTRANDE: You set fire to the Priest's barn? We're trying to live a quiet life and you set fire to the Priest's barn?

ARNAUD: It's what they expect of me.

BERTRANDE: You've destroyed the winter feed. For the whole village.

ARNAUD: It's what Martin would have done. If he'd found out.

BERTRANDE: We can't live as if we were young!

ARNAUD: Do we change?

Pause.

BERTRANDE: Maybe not in the end.

But I have a child. And if this one is born alive we have children.

We have children.

ARNAUD: What should I have done?

BERTRANDE: I don't know ... but I'm not sure that I can live with Martin any more.

A moment.

ARNAUD: I can barely live with myself.

BERTRANDE *and* **ARNAUD** *look at each other.*

BERTRANDE: *(To* **ARNAUD**.*)* Who are you?

ARNAUD: Who am I?

BERTRANDE: A murderer? A convict? A refugee? A traveller? A pedlar? A troubadour? A juggler? A bigamist? A bear?

ARNAUD: I'm your husband.

91

BERTRANDE: Are you?

ARNAUD: Who are you? A mother? A lover? An adulteress? A cook? A washerwoman? A butcher? A shepherdess? A storyteller?

BERTRANDE: I don't know.

I don't know who I am.

ARNAUD: You are Bertrande de Rols. Of the village of Artigat. And I am Martin Guerre. Your husband. Now we must invite everyone to the feast.

BERTRANDE: Père Raymond has them all under his thumb. He's telling everyone you're an imposter. No one wants to eat with us. The pig will rot in the yard.

ARNAUD: Then we'll dry the meat. We'll smoke it. We'll be eating sausages all winter. The baby will be born eating sausage.

BERTRANDE: Stop it!

Stop joking around!

ARNAUD: You used to like my jokes.

BERTRANDE: This isn't the time for jokes! They're angry. You'll be put on trial. If you're not who you say you are then you're an adulterer and a thief. Stealing their women. Stealing their money. Stealing their sheep. I don't even know the punishment for all that.

Pause.

ARNAUD: I can't win, can I?

If I'm not Martin I'm an imposter.

But the more I'm like Martin, the less you want me.

BERTRANDE: If you're not Martin, then I'm guilty too. I'm an adulteress.

ARNAUD: You're an adulteress anyway. You slept with the Priest.

BERTRANDE: We've all slept with the Priest.

Pause.

ARNAUD: Maybe it would be easier if I left.

BERTRANDE: You would leave?

ARNAUD: If you asked me to.

BERTRANDE: Maybe I want to be the one who leaves this time.

Maybe it's my turn to be someone else.

BERTRANDE wraps an animal skin round herself and leaves.

SANXI: I don't mind if you're my real father or not.

ARNAUD: I want to be a good father to you Sanxi.

SANXI: Grandfather said you were a loser.

ARNAUD: And where's Grandfather now?

SANXI: He's dead.

ARNAUD: There you go then. And what did he see in his lifetime? Nothing, that's what. From here to the market and back.

SANXI: What have you seen?

ARNAUD: Different countries. Different landscapes. Different food. Everything's different except people. People are the same everywhere.

SCENE 6

BERTRANDE *outside. She crushes apples. Enter* **ARNAUD**.

ARNAUD: Let me do that.

BERTRANDE keeps working.

ARNAUD: I'll do that.

She keeps crushing.

ARNAUD: Bertrande!

She stops.

ARNAUD: Let me do that.

BERTRANDE: No.

I really need to do this.

ARNAUD: We've plenty of cider for the feast.

BERTRANDE: You misunderstand.

I need to be doing this.

BERTRANDE *goes back to crushing.*

BERTRANDE: No pig.

(*Crush.*)

No cider.

(*Crush.*)

No feast.

(*Crush.*)

ARNAUD: Why not?

BERTRANDE *stops.*

BERTRANDE: The villagers are calling for a trial.

ARNAUD: I'm not denying it! I'll tell them I set fire to the barn.

I'll tell them why.

I'll tell them Père Raymond is Sanxi's father.

BERTRANDE: They don't believe you're Martin.

The orchard. The baby. Then the barn.

ARNAUD: It's what Martin would have done!

BERTRANDE: Perhaps they don't want you to be Martin.

Perhaps I don't want you to be Martin.

Perhaps Martin was right to leave.

ARNAUD: Well he's back now.

A moment.

ARNAUD: Come inside and we'll prepare for the feast.

BERTRANDE: You really think we can go on as if nothing has happened?

ARNAUD: We have to go on as if nothing has happened.

...

It's all we can do.

SCENE 7

Inside the house.

ARNAUD: We'll have walnuts. We'll have cheese. We'll have figs and honey.

BERTRANDE: If they won't eat with us it will all go to waste.

ARNAUD: Nothing will be wasted.

BERTRANDE: I'll chop, you peel.

They prepare the food.

BERTRANDE: Name?

ARNAUD: Martin Guerre.

BERTRANDE: Your parents were from the Basque country?

ARNAUD: Hendaye.

By the sea.

BERTRANDE: So your first language was Basque?

ARNAUD: I remember only a few words.

BERTRANDE: Yes?

ARNAUD: Ama.

BERTRANDE: And?

ARNAUD: Txakur.

BERTRANDE: Go on.

ARNAUD: Seme.

BERTRANDE: Yes.

ARNAUD: Seme.

And … alaba.

BERTRANDE: …

ARNAUD: Daughter.

Pause.

BERTRANDE: You say you are married to Bertrande de Rols

ARNAUD: I am married to Bertrande de Rols.

I've been married to her for seventeen years.

BERTRANDE: What was her dowry?

ARNAUD: Fifty pounds, a small vineyard, a bed with feather pillows, two sheets, a woollen blanket, a trunk and three dresses.

BERTRANDE: And which dress did she wear the day that you married?

ARNAUD: The blue.

BERTRANDE: It was the green.

The green's better in the rain.

ARNAUD: But it didn't rain.

BERTRANDE: There was a thunderstorm.

ARNAUD: After the ceremony. We were feasting in the barn.

BERTRANDE: It rained all morning on our wedding day.

ARNAUD: It doesn't matter! We just have to agree on this! We have to get our story straight. Or they'll never believe us! It doesn't matter if it's true … as long as we both tell the same story. It rained in the afternoon. You were in blue.

Pause.

BERTRANDE: I was in blue.

…

You had a son.

ARNAUD: Sanxi.

BERTRANDE: And were away for some years?

ARNAUD: Seven years.

BERTRANDE: When you returned … how did you recognise your wife?

ARNAUD: How did I recognise her?

BERTRANDE: How did you recognise her?

A moment.

ARNAUD: By her voice.

BERTRANDE: …

ARNAUD: By her smile.

BERTRANDE: …

ARNAUD: By the way our bodies remembered each other.

A moment.

ARNAUD: What will you say? About how you knew me.

BERTRANDE: The truth.

ARNAUD: What's the truth?

BERTRANDE: A slippery fish.

ARNAUD: What will you say?

BERTRANDE: I'll say that I knew you by your gait.

By your tread on the ladder.

By the scar on your leg.

By the tone of your voice.

By the strength of your hands.

By the smell of you.

By the way you eat your apples

SANXI *bursts in.*

SANXI: There are guards coming up the valley. I think they're from Toulouse.

BERTRANDE: Guards?

SANXI: They have hats with feathers.

BERTRANDE *looks at* **ARNAUD**.

BERTRANDE: You should leave.

ARNAUD: Leave?

BERTRANDE: They'll take you to Toulouse and you'll be put on trial.

You have to leave now. There's not much time. If you run. If you use the path the goats use. The high one.

ARNAUD: I'm not leaving.

BERTRANDE: If you're not Martin …

ARNAUD: I'm not leaving, Bertrande.

If I run again I have to keep running.

…

And I'm not young any more.

BERTRANDE: You're going to have to prove you're Martin.

ARNAUD: *(To* **SANXI**.*)* They're coming for me Sanxi. They say I'm not …

They say I'm not your father.

SANXI: If they don't believe you … what will happen to you?

ARNAUD: Nothing will happen to me.

SANXI: They're nearly at the big oak. The guards are nearly here.

…

They've got guns.

A moment. **BERTRANDE** *and* **ARNAUD** *look at each other.*

BERTRANDE: Run now!

ARNAUD: I'm not running.

BERTRANDE: What if you lose?

ARNAUD: How can I lose?
I am Martin Guerre.

Violent banging on the door.

A moment.

More banging

ARNAUD: Let them take me.

SANXI: *(To* **ARNAUD**.*)* You can't leave!

You'll ruin everything! Again!

(To **BERTRANDE***)* Don't let him leave!

Tell him he can't leave!

A gun is fired outside.

Banging on the door.

ARNAUD *leaves.*

A moment.

The cello speaks **SANXI**'s *line.*

SANXI: What will happen to him?

BERTRANDE: Nothing.

He'll be back.

SANXI: But will they believe him?

BERTRANDE: Of course they'll believe him.

SANXI: I've heard that if you steal a loaf of bread in Toulouse, they cut off your hand.

BERTRANDE: That won't happen to him.

SANXI: Will you have to go to Toulouse?

BERTRANDE: Yes. I'll go to Toulouse.

BERTRANDE *leaves.*

BERTRANDE *visits* **ARNAUD** *in the jail.*

SCENE 8

SANXI *and* **BERTRANDE** *at home.* **BERTRANDE** *is kneading bread.* **ARNAUD** *is not in the same space to start with.*

BERTRANDE: I'll send a loaf to the jail. The city bread is tasteless. And the water! No wonder they only drink wine. You've never tasted water like it. Everyone looks half dead. Perhaps it's the blue from the dye works.

SANXI: Is there anything good about the city?

She thinks.

BERTRANDE: On a clear day you can see the mountains.

SANXI: When will he be home?

BERTRANDE: Soon. He'll be home soon. Rose was up today.

BERTRANDE: *(As Rose.)* 'The size ae his feet. Ah kent him by the exact size ae his feet. He hus awfy wee feet for a big man.'

ARNAUD: *(As the Judge.)* 'The exact size of his feet.'

BERTRANDE: *(As Rose.)* 'Aye.'

ARNAUD: *(As the Judge.)* 'Why did you measure his feet?'

BERTRANDE: *(As Rose.)* 'Ma faither's the shoemaker.'

ARNAUD: *(As the Judge.)* 'Mafaethur?'

   (Turning to the bench.) 'Can we interview this man Mafaethur?'

BERTRANDE: *(As Rose.)* 'Mafaethur's ma faither ya bam. Whit's this trial costin? Whit a farce. Yiz ur pishin money doon the Garonne.'

SANXI: Did you see the bridge?

BERTRANDE: Still not finished. There's one perfect road in Toulouse. All cobbled. Leading to the river. But no bridge. They spent all winter trying to decide what to call it. They're calling it … 'The New Bridge'.

   Genius.

SANXI: When can I see him?

BERTRANDE: He's tired. And thin. Thinner than I remember.

   …

   Did you catch many fish?

SANXI: Who else was up today?

BERTRANDE: Père Raymond.

BERTRANDE: *(As Père Raymond.)* 'It's difficult to distinguish the essence of a man. What is essential? Is it the heart? The soul? The spirit?'

ARNAUD: *(As the Judge.)* 'You had a close relationship with the young Martin. You don't have to seek so far. There are other, more obvious features.'

BERTRANDE: *(As Père Raymond.)* 'Identifying features are the domain of the anatomists. I hear they make progress in this field. Perhaps one day we'll know more about it.'

BERTRANDE: Wanker.

SANXI: … ?

BERTRANDE: That was Rose.

That's what Rose said.

SANXI: Can't you tell who someone is just by looking at them?

BERTRANDE: Some say that he can't be Martin because Martin was taller and darker and had a flat nose.

Others say it's definitely Martin because he has the same broken tooth and the same scar on his leg …

SANXI: The one he got the day I was born.

Horses approaching. They both stop what they're doing to listen.

Enter **ARNAUD**.

A moment.

He goes to ruffle **SANXI**'s *hair.*

BERTRANDE *wipes her hands.*

She touches **ARNAUD**'s *face.*

BERTRANDE: You're back.

Pause.

BERTRANDE: What?

ARNAUD: They don't believe me.

BERTRANDE: Guilty?

ARNAUD: The house is surrounded. There are guards at the door.

BERTRANDE: Guilty?

ARNAUD: Of adultery, rape, theft and deception.

…

I'm to make amends before God in the chapel.

BERTRANDE: Then I'm guilty too.

ARNAUD: Bertrande … you're guilty of nothing. You believed I was your husband returned. You were deceived. A naïve woman, easily duped.

BERTRANDE: Easily duped?

ARNAUD: 'A lark in the hand is worth two on the wing.'

One husband is better than none.

They'll forgive you that.

BERTRANDE: What about you?

ARNAUD: *(Gently.)* I'm to be walked through the village, bareheaded and barefoot, and holding a burning wax taper. I'm to be shamed.

BERTRANDE: Shamed?

ARNAUD: I'm to be walked through the village to the big oak tree on the bottom path … where the gallows will be set up.

BERTRANDE: No!

ARNAUD: I'm to be hung. And my body is to be /

BERTRANDE: Enough!

A moment.

ARNAUD: Fetch the shirt that you sewed for me. The white linen. I'll wear that.

BERTRANDE: The shirt?

ARNAUD: With your stitching.

BERTRANDE: I don't know what shirt you're talking about.

ARNAUD: The night before I left, you finished a shirt. You put it in the trunk at the top of the ladder.

BERTRANDE: I did finish a shirt that night. And I put it in the trunk at the top of the stairs.

I didn't tell you that.

I'd forgotten all about it.

Banging on the door.

BERTRANDE: Who are you?

SANXI: He's my father.

ARNAUD: Fetch me the shirt.

A moment.

Banging on the door.

BERTRANDE *fetches the shirt, strips his old shirt over his head, and puts the white linen shirt on him.*

BERTRANDE: You're leaving again.

ARNAUD: If it's true what they say about blood being the soul of a person then I'll never leave again.

BERTRANDE: Everyone knows the blood isn't the soul. The breath is the soul. And it roams with the wind.

Banging on the door.

ARNAUD: I have to go.

SANXI: Don't go.

ARNAUD: I have to.

SANXI: Can't you escape?

ARNAUD: You can't escape from yourself.

ARNAUD *leaves.*

SCENE 9

*Griffon vultures are descending on **ARNAUD**'s corpse.*

BERTRANDE *shouts.*

BERTRANDE: Shoo!

She kneels by his body.

She sings.

SONG: Ar em al freg temps vengut: *(Azalais de Porcairagues.)*

Ar em al freg temps vengut

quel gels el neus e la faingna

el aucellet estan mut,

c'us de chantar non s'afraingna;

e son sec li ram pels plais

que flors ni foilla noi nais

ni rossignols no i crida

que l'am e mai me reissida.

SCENE 10

SANXI *and* **BERTRANDE**.

BERTRANDE *picks nits out of* **SANXI**'s *hair. He brushes her hand away.*

SANXI: Why didn't they believe him?

BERTRANDE: Our stories were too similar. Too complete. Truth is messy.

And unfinished.

Pause.

BERTRANDE: What story shall we tell the baby when she's born?

SANXI: There was this shepherdess who lived high in the Pyrenees,
looking after her flock.

Often, she would catch sight of a bear, stalking her flock from a
distance. He was a handsome bear, with a thick, glossy coat and a
muscular torso, arms and legs.

One day, she lured the bear with an injured sheep, captured him and
kept him with her all summer.

When winter came, he accompanied her back to the village. But
the villagers were suspicious of this hairy beast, and fearful for their
children and livestock. So they put him in the stocks and he was hung,
drawn and quartered.

Pause.

BERTRANDE: I don't think she'll like that one.

What about …

There was this shepherdess high in the Pyrenees. One day she lured
a bear with an injured sheep, captured him and took him home with
her.

Every day, she sent him out to bring back gifts … flowers, raspberries, honey, fragrant herbs, wild strawberries …

At first he resisted her advances, but bears have needs too.

Nine months later, a child was born, a tiny baby who nevertheless looked very much like her father.

Even at birth she had beautiful searching eyes.

And very hairy legs.

Pause.

SANXI: Will you always recognise me?

BERTRANDE: You're my son.

SANXI: If I went away for a few years, and came back … older. Maybe a bit taller.

Would you know it was me?

BERTRANDE: Where would you go?

SANXI: I don't know … say I went off to war.

BERTRANDE: If you went off to war you might not come back.

SANXI: To sea then.

BERTRANDE: If you went to sea I think you'd come back thinner.

SANXI: But would you know me?

BERTRANDE: Would you have lost any limbs?

SANXI: No.

BERTRANDE: Or any essential part of you?

SANXI: Essential?

BERTRANDE: Your nose for example.

SANXI: Let's say I have my nose

BERTRANDE: Then I think I'd know you.

Pause.

BERTRANDE: I should go and see to the sheep.

SANXI: Yes.

BERTRANDE *leaves.*

BERTRANDE *rounds up the sheep.*

BERTRANDE: Hup

...

Hup

...

Hup

...

SANXI *watches as she leaves.*

SANXI, *alone.*

END